THE SLEEP OF REASON

PHOENIX POETS

The Sleep of Reason

DAVID GEWANTER

THE UNIVERSITY OF CHICAGO PRESS
Chicago and London

DAVID GEWANTER, associate professor of English at Georgetown University, is the author of *In the Belly,* which won the John C. Zacharis First Book Award from *Ploughshares.* In addition, he is coeditor of *The Collected Poems of Robert Lowell,* and recipient of both a Witter Bynner Fellowship and a Whiting Writers' Award.

The University of Chicago Press, Chicago 60637
The University of Chicago Press, Ltd., London

Printed in the United States of America

12 11 10 09 08 07 06 05 04 03   1 2 3 4 5

ISBN: 0-226-28973-7 (cloth)
ISBN: 0-226-28974-5 (paper)

Library of Congress Cataloging-in-Publication Data

Gewanter, David.
The sleep of reason / David Gewanter.
p. cm.—(Phoenix poets)
Includes bibliograhical references.
ISBN 0-226-28973-7 (alk. paper)—ISBN 0-226-28974-5 (pbk. : alk. paper)
I. Title. II. Series.

PS3557. E897S57 2003
811′.54—dc21   2003044777

⊗ The paper used in this publication meets the minimum requirements of the American National Standard for Information Sciences—Permanence of Paper for Printed Library Materials, ANSI Z39.48-1992.

for Joy Young

I stand behind my contradictions

El sueño
de la razón
produce
monstruos

—GOYA, *Caprichos*

Contents

Acknowledgments

Grateful acknowledgment is made to the editors of the following periodicals and websites where these poems, or versions of them, first appeared:

Agni: "Jacopone: On the Cobbles," "Jacopone: The Scissors" (57, spring 2003)
Beltway: An On-Line Poetry Quarterly (washingtonart.com/beltway.html): "Convulvulus, a Lullaby," "Gag," "See Saw"
Berkeley Poetry Review: "Y"
Boston Phoenix: "Zero-Account" (17 January 2001)
Chicago Review: "Catullus VIII," "Divorce and Mr. Circe"
Georgetown Journal: "Cobbler's Children"
In Posse Review (www.webdelsol.com/InPosse): "Gag" and "Revenger Sonnet" in the Multi-Ethnic Anthology section; "Tacitus: City of Unseens" in the Attack on America section
Kenyon Review: "After the Wall" (n.s., 19, no.1, 1997)
Provincetown Arts Journal: "*Xenia:* Stranger/Guest"
Salamander: "One-Page Novel"
Slate (www.slate.com): "A is for Allegory," "The Loop: JFK Jr," "Marriage: Six Primers," "See Saw," "Traffic of Creations"
Tikkun Magazine: "*Chai:* 1924–2000"
Washingtonian Magazine: "A Lie-Awake Dirge"

Grateful acknowledgment is also made to the editors of books and websites that reprinted the following poems.

"*Chai:* 1924–2000" appeared in *Kiss Off: Poems to Set You Free,* edited by Mary D. Esselman and Elizabeth Ash Velez (Warner Books, 2003).

"Divorce and Mr. Circe," "One-Page Novel," and "*Xenia:* Stranger/Guest" appeared in *The New American Poets: A Bread Loaf Anthology,* edited by Michael Collier (University Press of New England, 2000).

"Divorce and Mr. Circe" (2000); "One-Page Novel" (2000); and "Zero-Account" (2002) appeared at *PoetryMagazine.com.*

*

My gratitude also to the Witter Bynner Foundation, the U.S. Library of Congress, and Georgetown University, whose fellowships allowed me time to write. Thanks also to my helpful and patient friends.

I

The sailors cried out, each to his god,
and flung their cargo overboard . . . .
But Jonah
went into the hold, lay down
and fell asleep.

—Jonah 1:5

A is for Allegory

Festooned in torn posters
for and against the *Contras,*
a new bookshop hires

slim dancers to perform:
two stalk in as
wind-up dolls,

each turning the other's key
yet turning it
less each time,

sapping its own strength
with helping, hobbled,
gimpy, stiffening . . .

then a third one
whirls from the aisle
marked *Health*

and cranks them
so they waddle and teeter
throughout the store,

silly signs
of promised creations,
past *Auto* and *Women,*

past *Family*
and not *Poetry*
while the third falls

from *Aging,* hands
on head, simon says,
a little crouching *a.*

See Saw

on which a boy, smiling
   at his friend stuck on
the raised end of the plank
hops off—his glee
to watch that boy drop:

Rage and delight, a sugar-bowl
   filled with salt. We need
a chump to cheer us
so God rubs Job with
brine, playing Satan

—but Job is too human
   cannot dance in pain
and make God happy
What joke is this
life you gave me?

Suffering grows
   a worm of delight
for those who watch,
the pitted eyes of Oedipus
make our play, worm

of BenGay squirted in
   your pants, burn your ass
Happy the ghoul
in ghoul's mask
handing the children apples

with razors inside, there's your trick
   or punch-line
obituary: "The farmer looped
a chain from tree to tractor,
drove off, and pulled it down

on his head." The woman arrested
   for resisting arrest,
Domine sing the doughty Monks
of Masoch, the man pinned
by a tree underwater,

giggling as his friend
   gives him mouth to mouth,
giggling, drowning, *Domine*
chant the monks, *Domine*
and smash their mouths

with boards—denying us
   our casual voodoo,
the pleasure to give pain
that gives pleasure of pain,
unmerited, cruel, free creation

in a falling world that falls
   but we kick it further—
the axe-man whispers *run*
to the convict he beheads
so the body for our delight

jumps up headless
   —a sick story
but undying, we
would empty Hell
for such life, whip

the mad dog for its
   palindrome
god dam, just kidding
just pulling your leg, you
hanging from the tree of Love.

After the Wall

People were hungry for books, for ideas, for art;
now we are smothered by the one we loved.
—Tadeusz Knowicki

The old artificers, underminers, and sappers
prinked in bearskin jackets and spatter-

dashes stand still, and toss their skull
caps faced with ciphers, their glazed leather and fall-

down linen—for the Wall has broken, and these,
the artificial and undermining metaphors dressed

for political warplay, are demobbed. Now the hooked eye
bleeds again, fatigues grow weary, and a pipe

is just a pipe. Once these paper troops shake
their meanings off, children paste their bodies in books,

so that Picasso's cockeyed horse noses Peter
Rabbit, and the Cat wears Kundera's hat; but even as matter

turns ductile and porous, there are new
chiselers grabbing chunks of the Wall, fusing

the fissures together again—they prop the swastika
on its skinny foot, sew an axe for Raskolnikov—

as children sleep the artisans force new sutures, so that
Godot comes to kill us, and Oedipus blinds his mother, so that

race-baits, blacklists, and figures of cruelty sell
like relics or baseball cards in the aisles of Century Hall . . . .

Gag

"It was just your type of dream,
jumpy, a movie out-take
   where

the masked surgeon drags
his son to the operating
   theatre

and hands him a scalpel
saying, *Kid, it's never too late
   to learn . . .*

the guy under the sheet
is beaming, his eyes watery
   with pride,

So nice of you, he murmurs,
My children ignore me—:
   bashful,

the kid knifes him open, blood
blooms on the sheet,
   the pulpy

red of borscht, too red
for real life, it's just a
   borsht-belt

gag . . . except that
when the director yells
   Cut

You're killing 'em
no one, not even the body
   sitting up

cracks a smile, so the joke
keeps looping the set, a kind
   of intestine . . .

when comics need new gags
they squeeze their families
   for material,

squeeze till something nasty
pops out—: It isn't
   cinéma vérité,

more like a steamboat
burning its cabin-planks
   for fuel:

Should we call it art
just because real people
   get hurt?"

Jacopone: The Scissors

Yellow ditches, broken turf, the wheel-rutted
farmroads creasing the hillsides of Todi
  are mossed

with pollen, cut flowerheads, olive pits,
the living shroud of spring *(Says the Poet . . .)* —
  Grit drops

from God cleaning His hands, the ancient Work
on us done . . . . Which road do we take now?
  The knobbed

cantering donkey of Appetite
halts at the corner: *via dolorosa*
  or *via media,*

God's golden mean
weighs us against the angels—:
  Daily I am told

to love my neighbor—but huddled
inside my love is a loathing for his
  filthy life,

the brawling, drunken parties, swaying women,
his thumping bed—and so my love, the gift
and issue

from Heaven's fingers, has flowered in me
as hate . . . and so I am commanded to honor
the Sin of rage—

There is no middle path now,
no escape in sophistry, self-hatred,
crafted

confession: I stand here begging,
flailing at my head, the mulish
Fool of God

braying at farmers to stop,
starving myself for "my own good,"
my face dirtier

than my wife's gravestone—:
What a parody of sainthood, this
Schoolman's mumble,

the sad, lethal puns of my poetry—
"God's mean, God is mean . . . ."
Day after day

a trash of gold, the fume and haze of pollen
greasing the sun. The choke of fertility is
upon us,

His fingers scissor my ribcage—
fingers too tired to crack a shell
    or let it drop.

II

"Heave me overboard," said Jonah,
"and the sea shall be calm to you."
But the sailors cried
to the Lord, "Do not compel us to kill
an innocent man—for it was You, by Your will,
who brought this about . . ."

—Jonah 1:12, 14

Cobbler's Children

The fireman bedevilled
by the smokeless house

the lawyer silenced
by his sinless wife

the General spoiling
for a crabapple kid

the shoes of the cobbler
go homeless;

the priest sells airspace
above his Church

an ounce of prevention
is a pound of flesh

the Quaker killing
a whale for God

Father, how like you
this likeness—;

a stitch in time
heals no wounds

the fireman is fired
for criminal arson

burn your bridges
at both candles

the children cobble
their tongues at home.

Xenia: *Stranger/Guest*

their own flesh and blood
and tinctures natural

—Herrick

I count your quick life by minute, day, and year,
  or by the tremble your head-pit makes
beneath our shrinking family tree, where no son
    meets his grandfather
and fungus soaks the heartwood to molasses—
    One night   you plucked

the forewaters and made your mother groan, crawling
  backward from bed under a Hercules
of pain, will, nails in my arm as you hiccupped
    a first prank, knotting
your purple tie neatly round your throat,
    Joy's curtain   of flesh

parting on the near-suicide: we held your
  pink prune face, held you like a torah packed
with nitro. Cuckoo-boy, you muscled others
    from the clotting test tube
till only your heart-light flashed the screen . . . .
    Could I be   all father

and fill the line, not wince when you call everyone
  Dada, stumbling after strangers . . . as I once
stalked across the green linoleum, a baby
    Frankenstein reaching for hands
that pulled back to make me lurch further,
    Anger   Absurdity

my Janus-parents, the house of *in loco,*
  meaning rewoven in the day's
shuttling luck—until any moment
    means anything. The Book
of Home reads *Praise* one day
    and *Blame*   the next:

we write yours with "no" and "don't"
  and "wait": yet you'll become its hero.
Maybe some stranger clouded in the woods
    will touch you—a love beyond ours—
and so, disguised by love, you'll cleave
    your way   to your wife.

—That was Odysseus, flanked by father and son,
  chopping down men. Your son may not meet me
(we tear our books) but show him this mottled tree.
    Wands of the tree-men have jizzed the roots,
it should grow on the day of my death.
    So (I pray)   should you.

Chai: *1924–2000*

for Yehuda Amichai

Page of sand, scab-flakes of ink;

page of sand, page of skin:
where are you now?

On the tongue, life is a verb
and death, a proverb:
Apple eats apple-blossom,

seed eats the apple . . . .
Your name, in the macaroni
of tongues, Ah-me-*hide,*
foreign and sentimental

as the pendant *Chai*—life—
noosing the ancients of St. Pete
waiting for the Early Bird Special

—or the girls in Bolinas
you saw loosening

their tefillin-strap

bikinis: souls
opening and closing,

a prayer drifting everywhere
but up—
Proverbial waves lap

a beach of crumbs.
Letters swirl in fat broth,
a name is lifted to the lips;
waiters wipe

the clock face clean.
Drop the page,
come out. *Come out:*

the body is an apple
to the seed,

the body is a seed in the earth.

Tacitus: City of Unseens

The old Annals bored me, a wheezing chronicle of softhanded pander-priests: the fragrant meats and oils, potions to plump a husband, gutted rabbits dictating a future we already know . . . not a word for God. Better to write of the flesh, spirit swallowed up in the body, a dagger

II

bedded in the chewing ox. Will my *Annals* slice good from evil? A history should read like morality, poetry, epic . . . but ours was a mean, obsequious age, monotonous downfalls dangling from monotonous causes. In the Senate, a son prosecuted his father for treason—both were

III

named Vibius Serenus, the docket read as if one placid man attacked himself. From the shores of Capri, whirlpools of sedition flushed the eye of Caesar. Men stooping to pray clutched nooses to their breasts . . . Vibulenus Agrippa, libeled in the Senate, stood before his peers and

IV

gulped poison: they dragged his body to jail anyway and strangled the corpse. The gods must laugh at our misery, their tears of glee freezing the crest of Olympus. Even Tiberius marveled at the chaos he caused; a new astrologer was brought nightly to his cliff-garden, to "advise him" . . .

V

but though he demanded flattery, Tiberius loathed the man who spoke it: on the path back his slave hurled each of them into the sea. One sage was spared, a paranoid who always predicted his own imminent death; for once, he was right—how Caesar trusted him after that!

VI

The house of Rome, a honeycomb of vengeance: new words, new rooms built for reprisals even as the old ones dripped with life. Sejanus never became Emperor, but he suffered an emperor's death—the whole family wiped out: his daughter cried to the hangman, *"What have I done?*

VII

I won't do it again—punish me with a beating, like other children!" Our sacred laws forbid the execution of virgins: the hangman first had to violate her, the ropes waiting beside them; then her strangled body was thrown down the Gemonian steps, twice killed. In ancient days, it is said,

VIII

savage man lived in peace: since then we have shaped ourselves as beasts; chroniclers tell of women giving birth to owls, or stunted deer; even the phoenix, flying in splendor from Egypt, so appalled the birds nearby they fell to the sea dead. History, to sound like poetry? Devotions

IX

sung to the deaf. Our curses continued, bland Heaven watching all: in Fidenae, an ex-slave built a shabby amphitheatre for gladiatorial shows—starved for amusements, whole families swarmed up the stands . . . suddenly the structure collapsed, crashing outward

X

and inward, flowing over the crowd. Some found the kindness of quick death, but scores of others lay mangled among the stone and timbers—frantic, their kinsmen could see and hear them, but could not pull them out. Days and nights passed . . . there they sat, still talking with the victims,

XI

until at last no moan or answer came from the ruins. When the rubble was cleared, they rushed to hug and kiss the corpses, quarreling over faceless remains. Thus disease spread through Fidenae: fifty thousand perished. Why read of Romulus, Theseus? A theatre, a city, stained rocks,

XII

a tomb . . . banalities make our epic. What else . . . Lucius Calpurnius Piso: he died a natural death, a rare end for one so distinguished. Son of a man whose censorship I have recorded, he won an honorary Triumph in Thrace, and lived to eighty. —Moderate, tight-lipped, despite irresistible

XIII

pressure from corrupt nobles . . . accused of moderation, I suppose— What more is there to write? A windpipe can be stretched and stretched, till flesh must beg for the blade. All these men, evil and good, are dead: I owe it to their

ancestors
and to their children

now strolling the leafy avenues
of this quiet city, not to

name them here.

Catullus VIII

Clinton, Oval Office, 1999

"Even while you play the clown,
   sad Catullus,
you see what's lost. Now learn from it.

Bright remembered
days, spent sniffing after my mistress;
   no one loved
as much as I loved her, cream,
   games, lust
given to her, who never loved me

   less— Now she loves you
no longer, Catullus—you limp, brooding clod:
   quit *snivelling*
after her, and let her flit away. Brace yourself:
   you must not break.

And so, dear girl, *bonne chance*—
   Catullus is stiff,
though he won't come uninvited. As for you,
   you'll regret this,
looking out for company, looking out till dawn . . .

how will you survive?
There's no one to call your love-name;
Who will you kiss?
There are no lips to nibble

while
Catullus, grim in resolve, stands here
unbroken."

One-Page Novel

Kind, almost courtly, a "good listener," he kept lovers
away, fearing and feeling that long contact would reveal

some horrid prospect of his interior—and though his soul
had stilled like seawater left in a tank, he kept his dread

as a keepsake, caring more for it than for the woman
who pressed herself against his arm at work, breathing . . .

so that finally, when he met a dark-eyed misanthrope, whose
severe answers to men masked her own fear of exposure, of

letting her nature mix with theirs, he thought she discovered
his hidden self, like a gleaner in a field of glass gems

who, knowing the small profit in some glittering cast-off,
still pockets it for another day: what a *frisson,* he told

himself, to be seen at last, seen through, to be found wanting
and still wanted. He took her sourness for sympathy, criticism

for care. And she, sensing that withheld affection somehow
contented him, knew he'd never press her to the wall:

whether a man thinks too much of himself, or too little,
the woman is left alone. How well their love was paid

for what it gave away,   a damp valley now blackening
beyond the smudge-lamps   of their terrace. Flanked

on the love seat,   they hug a family of stratagems
while the lost coin   of the sun rolls over

the stronghold of houses,   over the reckless sea,
then gilds other houses   then rolls away . . . .

Je reste roi de mes douleurs,   I remain king of my sorrows.

Divorce and Mr. Circe

When, my quiet scientific friend,
    fattening your rabbits for the blood-tap,

        the smirking pig trotting toward its noose,
did you first think of grafting a new life

to your life? Because the body is hostile
    (you once explained) it must be tricked

        into welcoming the foreign substance
that can save it, the trickle of pig

you now slip inside a man's brain. Call it
    immuno-suppression. Or call it

        a violation of self, when the spores
leech through the soft Parkinsonian

ganglia, so the spastic man,
    tied twenty years to a chair by

        his frantic wife, can now smack
a nine iron and snort *Watch her go* . . . .

To graft new life is to cut one away,
    to grow from withering—

Whatever it is you put into a brain
has first come from yours:

What remains there today
when dog will mew, and cat will

have his day, when a man
quivering after years of

deliberation rises from his chair at last,
closes with steady hand the door

his wife holds
and walks away from his house?

Marriage: Six Primers

1. *Hole in the eye*

   When she hears his father's accent she learns
what he suppressed. He sees in her mother's hallway
the decor she hates. Between them, a balance
scale weighted MOTHER FATHER YOU ME
—the loads shifting image by image.
   A mother left in the car.
   The father's bottom teeth.
And the small deductions—yearbook photos,
hidden cigarettes, names said dreaming,
his taste, the pills sent in the mail—
   As if a sailor squinted for land so long
the sun burned holes in his eyes;
standing in his house, he jerks his head
this way and that, just to see it sidelong . . . .

2. *The shuttle*

Lover and beloved.
   Who carries the most desire?

Better to ask who eats the apple,
   the pig or the family roasting it—

Or ask the two woodsmen
  on the shuttle toy

chopping the wood they're made of;
  or the samurai and geisha

pumping mechanically—a perfect fit—
  cock and cunt sliced from one stone.

3. *eppur si muove*

Rising from the altar of promises, he sees
  a tearful lover in the church. She cries

in relief; he feels it as grief. And though
  kissing his bride, he silently swears, like Galileo

telling the Inquisitors yes, my Earth
  anchors the universe—

and yet (rising from
  below) *she moves all the same.*

4. *Duet of days*

She: After this many years, I test positive! Week eight—
He: You—that makes it mid-March: I was gone all that month.

*

She: . . . so Jeff was in town then, and we drank a lot and . . . .
He: You'd better call him up: that's his kid you're carrying, not mine—

*

She: What's with these condoms? Who did you bang on that trip?
He: . . . so I never, never meant to hurt you. One night she and I smoked dope . . . .

*

—On Thanksgiving they learn the baby began on Valentine's;
they teach her numbers, the stars, and animal sounds.

5. *I stand behind my contradictions*

—J. Y.

At first glance you were tall, tall! Birch
  yellow hair, piano fingers. And short a dime.
I felt something in my pocket, handed you
  ten thoughts (of bed). We split

a pizza, then split from everyone—
  our lovesick summer, bedridden as invalids.
Now the doctor shows me my sperm—
  "Too many pinheads" (the doctor,

trained in mechanical reproduction).
  But here, our shining boy . . . .
A swallowed dime could kill him.
  When his chin shakes with cold

I start to sweat. And when
  the homeboys gather, you moon them
(behind curtains), sing "Vertigo"
  to the tune of *Camelot*—

charms and dangers to spell our home.

6. *Dice*

They fit snug sleeping, their nipples make dots
  on dots. Blockheads, but the sum of our parts.

All day they bump each other around,
  two faces avoiding the one fate. Suddenly thrown

for a loss: *snake eyes.* Shaken to their bones, rubbed
  and pleaded with, tumbling through

a glitter of choice—till their number's up,
  and the raker finds the die.

Or What You Will

Stories take place only when they're told,
    a child's
  Once upon a time of no time

or place,
a silent movie replayed in the music

of our day, romance heard instead
    as comedy,
  chattering newsreel, droning

divorce case—
softened, made up, two actors hug

and caress languorously, their lips purse
    on film
  even though they really chitchat

about dinner,
or simply insult each other. . . .

What is there to say now? You two
    have splintered,
  but your one past has ingrown

so that any
memory of marriage becomes

a divorce-plot heroically fought off
        or, finally,
    embraced. And now the actuaries

of love
nod their heads, watching the futures

of last night falter at dawn, the rosy
        fingered
    dawn, bloodnails of cut buds,

the staggered
daylight that rights itself before

we can wash for breakfast.
        When
    did it fall apart? the relatives

tsk tsk,
Can't you two make up?

Story of makeup, story without
        make up:
    only one draft refreshes your family,

hiking long ago
(or now) to Lobster Cove, past the frayed

saltwash robber mansions
        that own
    the Maine beaches to the tidemark,

the squinting
dowagers so full of trusts they suspect

the four of you wading by, asking you
        And you would be . . . ?
    At the harbor cafe, sea-bells

drone
to no one, mulching crates

rinse the fish head breeze—
        Chicken lobster
    that season, cheap as chicken,

shells
so soft even the children

crack them, wagging the freckled
        claw meat
    vises before their folks—

a dumb-show
that can mean *whatever,*

whatever you want, a fable
        drawn in sand
    or butter, a script of futures

you spend
nights reading in your palm.

Zero-Account

for my sister

Your "x," withdrawn, vengeful,
undertakes the spousal

rip-off. Quivering passion,
once negated, murders love—

Kindness? "Justice"
is how greed frames
every divorce:

cupid's backstabbing
alphabet.

Convolvulus, a Lullaby

The Convolvulus means "Bonds. Uncertainty."

Yet it's the Pink Convolvulus,
pink flowers, a color like yours, that says

"Worth, sustained by judicious
and tender affection"—
so
let me lace the Clematis
("Mental beauty")

round the stout Corn Cockle that stands for
"Duration, Gentility." And then
I'll take Crowsfoot, that

Stop this. What are you up to? You're just
quoting from The Language of Flowers:
try singing to me without a book—

We sang Ethel Merman,

we got evicted; sticky pants,
flesh sore, soured and

blear from coffee, we
strolled the Taj Mahal
houseboat
near Caffé Trieste—:
you asked me for my story

but dozed off before 'puberty';
so I brought you flowers, Abatina
("Fickleness") and Zinnia

—I remember Zinnia: "Thoughts of absent
friends." Pretty words drowned
in a vase. I'm sleepy. Tell me about guar gum—

Guar, the noblest

of gums, left his hearty
band of food supplements

to find his family: cousin Spirit
the alcoholic, cousin Bubble,
chewed up,
stomped on the sidewalk—
Guar smashed Spirit's head,

the leaking brains pried
Bubble up, but he was tasteless
and never thanked Guar,

who sank back to his corn mix,

back to his   his   corn futures
(are you asleep yet?)

back to Corn Straw,
"Agreement,"
                    and the petals
of Volkmannia,
flower that reads like

Madmen
but spells
"May you be happy."

Redd-Pound Slamma

or, "Fear and Apathy Kept Joe Redd at St. E's
Long After He Should Have Gone Free"
—*Washington Post,* April 8, 2001

Nobody has read Joe Redd
till we read in the paper
that he fell on his head,

fell on his head at ten
and never seemed himself again,
grew "epileptic," a word

his mother never said,
but heard from doctors

who measured his head,
trying to fit his fits,
Joe, laughing in

the city
of no name,
a preposition, "The District of —"

he was
        pre-positioned
for violence—the doctor

wrote, *If they try to kill him*
he's going to try to kill them.
O Dr. Eye to Eye,

you should have read
the stars instead—:
                        So, in 1968,

just as Dr. King was shot,
Joe Redd got his number and cuffs
at St. Elizabeths

Hospital, DC,
sea of tranquility . . .
Never tried for a crime,

Joe served 32 years, a
beautiful baritone
showing visitors around,

"Here's where Ezra Pound
slept," that poet
never tried for a crime,

who sang, in
Fascist Italian
opera, that

Jews should die:
jewing the Jew
and Jewkin alike—

Old Ez, old father
play-acting the Dada trial
by lying on the floor,

a recumbent
mannequin, they said,
the doctors, hiding his crime

in medical prose—
When Pound got arrested
he told his shrink

I broke—my head,
Ez, Ez, we theorize
his head, he never plead

but sat 12 years,
got laid and fed,
never met Joe Redd:

for nobody theorized Joe Redd,
till we read in the paper
that he fell on his head,

a catacomb city
above which the Cosmonaut,
bubbled in
his space station,

circled the earth
so long his country
collapsed beneath him—

Doctors, they should have read
the stars instead of giving
Joe pills and shots,

telling themselves that he
"kept himself here,"
scared of what he might do

if free, do what's in his head
or what's in yours,

two ideas for one life,
one was crazy, the other
was his, and he never said—:

"We gave him a choice,
  We gave him a chance,
He's no James Joyce,
  He dropped his pants . . ."

So Joe Redd got
educational therapy,
psychotherapy,

industrial and
dance therapy,
rap, skat,

and poetry—
got three hot
meals and a cot,

got whatever life
kept him out of ours
until . . . it was noticed

he was not
crazy—
so now

he's out! he's anywhere,
his thick, innocent belly
and cockeyed gait,

he now sleeps late,
learns the ZIP codes,

and counts his change—

Break your head,
the world comes in:

Which of us should be
in or out of St. E?
—depends on your poetry . . .

There was this lady fell on her head,
gave birth to the Laureate Pinsky;
there was a girl sent

Pound her rhymes, he said
They lack obliquity
so she wrote

Madwoman in the Attic instead—

A neurologist wrote poems,
learned the ropes,
gave the walking dead

L-Dopa,
saw them float like butterflies
then stuck them in a book

you can pay to read—
But poets,
the unknown rulers,

a Pope, a Bishop, and two Moore,

drove past Redd
to visit Ezra, at St. E,
they scribbled about

the world of books gone flat—

Who pays the price
for bad ideas?
                    —did we
let the pure products
of America go free?

This is a world of books gone flat—

This is the Jew in a newspaper hat,

seeing
the *Post* stick it
to Joe Redd, whose face

the photos never show,
swollen hands, a sallow eye,
the balding back of a head

and, in the last shot,
the gospel diners
rise to their feet

Heaven
they sing, facing him
O praise him, praise him

—and us reading, mouthing
in reverse,
Pray it's him

Sweet
Lord of Injustice,
pray that it was only

done to him.

A Lie-Awake Dirge

sung to the "Sailor's Hornpipe"

Oh   it's
heroin for guns, and guns for hostages,
opium in China for teacups in London,
it isn't a crime, it's only state policy,
diamonds for napalm, and butter for bribes.

It   was
General General General Motors
who built lots of planes for the Army and Air Force,
that shot down the Germans and bombed out the plants
where Opel was building the Luftwaffe planes.

And   yet
General Motors owned some of Opel
and met them in Lisbon to talk over business
and business was good for bombing each other
because the two countries paid them in advance.

So while
GM products bombed GM-linked factories
and slave-workers died and the managers fled
yet most of the company would surely survive
(unless the Russians took over Berlin).

And now
it's General Electric who wires the bomb
that shorts the grid and blacks out Belgrade
who hands up Slobo to get World Bank loans—
to pay for GE to build a new grid.

Because
it's never a crime if the market is free
and opium in China buys judges in London
and Exxon supports the PBS programs
that show us how Exxon won't pay for its spills.

So it's
Opel that sues, as a civil corporation,
for damage we did to their Luftwaffe plants;
and GM paid Congress to pay them and pay them,
—a *Golden Treasury* that verse can't reverse.

Revenger Sonnet

Achilles, dragging Hector's corpse
round the dusty plains of Troy, grew bored.

—Iliad, XXIV

"Hitler hugged the Volkswagen—but he also
   called Henry Ford his hero, nailed his photo
   above his desk, got him a medal too.
Corn we eat grows from shit. The man who

invented the electric can opener
   gives the Aryan Nation millions a year:
   does every opened can kill a Jew? Once,
I sublet my place to a Dresden student

(nice kid), and panicked: would my Nazi books
   upset him? I boxed them up, *Auschwitz, Speer,*
Nuremberg . . . German shame had become mine:

we'd never square things. —Bothered me all year,
   a stew rattling the lid. My neighbors took
him to church, gospel ladies clapping time,

the clink-clink as his change hit the plate . . . ."

Jacopone: House

Concrete foot dripped from a barrel,
  a keystone that fits no door; spackle,
  horsehair, and newspulp

  firm this house in which
    LOVE is locked:

Its home-birth staggers the waiting soul
  that falls gasping, soul whose groans
  and panic drain from the house,

  puddling from lintel and downspout
    onto the champing gravel

where now stoop the chalky
  moonflesh lovers, outlyers dabbing
  chilled fingers and foreheads clean

of dissolution—nightly they huddle at
  the ditch, servile

and expectant, yet this house
  makes domestic no man
  or woman, its entries are

  caulked and braced against them . . .

Bound and silent LOVE, *treasure held beyond the reach of thieves—*

Suppliant lovers, the candles you cup
  burn your hands, secrets wheeze
  from your clamped mouths;

  the gifts that belly your satchels—
    unguents and molded glass,

baubles from Chair City, Knife City—
  have pried open gates, curtains, legs . . .
  until now: House, silent as

  a frozen ship, crystalline blue
    under

a thin, coppered rainbow—
  Wordless and exhausted is
  the soul attendant on LOVE,

  and happy to be sealed inside
    the countinghouse,

dried of desire—to be the happy clam
  displayed forever before LOVE
  the famished Lodger,

  whose scrupulous hands cool
    the bone china,

whose throat is stoppered against flesh and tears and sound . . . .

Y

Nearly all my mother's friends are widows (a comment on her marriage). One, a professor, told her how nice the West Side Y in Manhattan was, a real bargain, close to Central Park and Lincoln Center. *The Met,* breathed my mother hearing this, as memories of her girlhood crimes surged upward, when she snuck through the stage door of the Opera House by reciting French lessons with a friend:

La lune blanche
luit dans les bois

she sang. And Miriam answered,

de chaque branche
part une voix
sous la ramé . . .
O bien-aimé

Then they laughed in French, and pranced past the doorman, who took them for sopranos in the chorus. Even though she did this in the Old Met, long since torn down, she booked a room at the Y and took her crinkled snippet of the Old Met's lurid *Curtain of Gold* along for luck. She held it out to me like a saint's bone as I picked her up from the train.

My mother at the Y. Its pale facade flaked a manna of plaster on the bum lolling atop the sidewalk steam vents. Bolted above this grating was a spiked lattice of girders to prevent anyone lying there—airspace being a prized commodity even at street level, if the air was warm. But this man had jerry-rigged a hammock from the window-grilles; there he slept, a coldsore Damocles above his bed of nails.

The lobby's low-vaulted ceilings sagged between pillars—once, a Spanish Cloister motif; now, overlit and forbidding, a postcard from a trip you can't remember. When my mother focussed on the Puerto Rican tilers chipping and chatting by the snack machines, and the Bed-Sty basketball team, a dozen splendidly built and languidly sullen black buzzcut teens tossing a ball between the couches, she experienced immediate race-panic. "Oh God, we're calling the St. Moritz," she whispered. $198. And full. Mom meanwhile began negotiations with the desk clerk: "Well, can you refund my deposit on account of family illness?"

But there was nowhere else to go, and after finding out about the Y's pottery classes and ping-pong tables, my mother began to mellow, and we bundled her things into the narrow, severely cleaned dormer on the tenth floor. All along the hall we heard instruments being played, violins, cellos, each following a different part behind a closed door. Juilliard students were cramming for finals, and my mother was enchanted. "All this culture—for $37.50 a night! Don't sit yet honey, I'll check for bugs."

We talked until dark, when the buildings set their Lego silhouettes against the winter skyline. I could see how her face was beginning to resemble her father's, losing its distinctiveness as our family features slowly articulated themselves: the eyes had grown milky and flat, and my grandfather's long-dead frown lines creased the parchments of her cheeks. She was full of impossible plans to walk to Lord & Taylor's Christmas windows—with her ankles, a crawl to Compostella. "And the big tree above the skaters at Rockefeller Center, what a sin to miss it." I began to appreciate the delicate passage she was making, from adulthood to old age, leaving the larger world for the charmed places of girlhood. Forgetfulness lent her innocence—the crises of that afternoon were long past, and she was planning to meet "some of the music-girls on the hall. You go on, and we'll shop all day tomorrow." I'd been itching to leave for hours, but now the thought of her wandering guilelessly around the building seemed just as much of an anchor. And yet, relieved and fretful, I kissed her goodbye.

The elevator stops at every floor: 9—lights flickering; 8—"Mario" brings his mop and pail on board; at 7, an old man shuffles vaguely forward, bristled and frumpy, his freckled head dented softly by new fontanelles. A clean vinyl coat, custard smooth, sized for a larger man. Mario and he chat like veterans about the elevator until the janitor murmurs, "Hey Mr. Jeffrey my man, better repack your gear there, don't want the chicas getting ideas," and Jeffrey notices his open zipper, and what I have been staring at since he got on. "Oh Christ," he mumbles as Mario winks at me, and soon they resume their complaints about the elevator as we drop sluggishly, 4—dark offices; 3—door jammed closed, someone swearing behind it.

I felt sick entering the cavernous antiseptic lobby; too late to take her anywhere else . . . no place was safe, besides dragging her after me . . . . Jeffrey started a dreary interchange with the security guard while I loitered by the door; the night air slicing inward smelled cold and unclean, that odd city freshness.

The guard touched my arm. "Listen pal, I can't leave my desk, but you're going out—how's about taking Jeffrey here to the corner deli; it's over on the left, and one of them will bring him back. Whadaya say?" Jeffrey kept his eyes down, he lived in the passage my mother had come to. And he was pulling me after him, he and Mom, pulling me to that place where the child takes charge of a parent—where they exchange childhoods. And, as if speaking meant making a choice, I left my mother to the girls she hadn't met yet, helped the old man plod across the street, and then ran off to find my friends.

Traffic of Creations

1. *Thrift, Horatio, Thrift*

His nuptial poems,
so loving they moistened

every listener's eye
and seat, did coldly

furnish forth cash
for his alimony payments.

2. *"Don't go down on any bunny"*

Ski-masked
axe-wielding

antivivisectionists
chop down lab doors, freeing

100 grey rabbits
caged for research

and infected with
herpes. "How do you

keep safe from
herpid rabbits?"

3. *Frozen Margarita*

Meeting monthly at Pizza Hut
the *CryoGenic Support Group*
talks the new technology, how

someday a sleepless
gearhead Dr. F
will cure their deaths,

regenerating the whole,
now diseaseless body or
(for the economically

minded) just
the blanched, nitrogenized
head, severed and preserved—

Tonight it's the poor
who live best, their
dispensable torsoes

fatted like Balzac:
head-only Harry, dreaming
to be sutured

to a Charles Atlas
orders pepperoni, double cheese,
and stout;

but for full-body
Bertha the flesh is a temple,
rigid debutante waiting for

its white-suited date:
“Veg Sampler, please,
and lite beer—”

Meeting at the next table,
Adult Children of Parents.

The Loop: JFK Jr

Graveyard anchormen bumble
their script: *he was—he is—he was*
lost? Watching the watchers, looking for
  an absence, old footage
  running the treadmill—

a bride-in-waiting paces her room.
We have adopted your orphan boyhood,
gape as you salute the rolling horizon
  of your father's box, too young to grieve,
  and later, too politic to run for office.

Elect, unelected, scandalously
temperate—no one was bruised
by your heel. You hoped to climb
  down Rushmore
  (every woman would give you a landing)

your uxorious breath, a white gauze
sopping the bloodsport, Camelot. Only you
could call Washington's zoo-pit of celebrity
  George: easy to bare your teeth
  for cameras aimed at your head.

Flying tonight you squint the horizon,
drained light will steady the hand:
veer right . . . what is correct? . . . then right again,
   then left . . . . The sky bewilders a level head,
   shreds a plane to confetti—

Alchemical sea washing film from the eye.

III

And so they heaved Jonah overboard,
and the sea stopped raging.

—Jonah 1:15

Jacopone: On the Cobbles

The sons of drunks and suicides
never trust the State,

they nurse any idea
that topples a powerful man—;
yet a husband
                    who sees his wife truly,

but too late,
never trusts Love:
unless he exiles his body

he lives to break women
and break his vows
to God.

My fancy life, fancy wife,
poetics of a grand style
fluttering
               above Hell

where Simon, the corrupt
counsel, teeters,
gullet stuffed
with flesh . . . .

Here's poetic justice
for a lawyer:
one night I dressed

my wife Vanna in finery
for the theatre,
pulled her
                satin bodice down

to show my jewels;
bella donna, wide-eyed,
birdlike, sinless, vacant—

cream worked into the shoulders,
petals crushed for

her throat, sweet breasts;
Let me dine with you
she pleaded;

No, I said, *at midnight*
let us dine
                on each other—

I sent her to the show;
there, the stands

collapsed and crushed her—
dressed by me for death . . .

I ran, I carried her groaning,
unlaced
            her corset

to find beneath
a blood-drenched hair-shirt.

The trestle had crushed
her ribs, but the scratches—
those she had given herself.

"Signor avvocato"
moaned her handmaid
as I shook her,
"she . .

the lady, had always asked
our Holy Father to mortify her—

she wore that shirt
every day, everywhere
but to bed."

Now, crawling through the Square
day and day and night—

street-boys prod me,
the droll lawyer
is reborn

Jacopone,
God's Maniac:
a birth from a death—

now I leave meat in my stable
to rot, dandle a rosary
of maggots;

the slackbellied Franciscans
live a *soft life*—
                                    Some days

my old clients creep toward me,
a filthy beggar broken-kneed
on the cobbles of Todi—

Perdono, Sr Benedetti,
their soft hands and voices,

Perhaps you remember me?
Maybe you have now finished my Will?
The stench appalls them.

Body, may it
sting the nostrils
                                    of God—

Love mankind
I say in my *Lauds,*

But don't trust your senses:
to satisfy eye, cock, or tongue
is to become a beast.
                                    Here

the fields of sunflowers
turn from the sun:
a jailer must
                    beat himself . . . .

My wife betrayed me
for God,
          the Gentleman

who watched the ladies
watch a spectacle,
whose Fingers idly
held their chairs
                    aloft

awhile:
who scrawled
onto Vanna's body
a love letter,
                    charge

of piety
in foolscap and blood,
runic scabs,
light stroke, scar . . .
                              all of it,

all but me—
blotted out for good.

Hocus Pocus

"—I'm inconsolable at the present time,
said Mariah Carey,

I was a very good friend of Jordan,
he was probably the greatest

basketball player this country has ever seen . . ."

*

After naming the beasts, we borrowed back
the words,

little grace, little hocus pocus,
blood diary muttering *me me me*—

person, place, spoken thing,
bits of us

drift off, stick to whatever people say,
tall Dr. Ångström trapped within

his pinhead Å, Mr. Graham
mashed up as

Graham crackers. Must the body grow
inside words? Is Cassius Clay? Adam Ant?

Our natures are bent on defying
   the fates

in our names, let Jonathan not be
Swift, nor Oscar Wilde . . . .

Yet the mob grieving for Caesar
   happily ripped

the poet Cinna—they couldn't find
Cinna the Senator, and his name

fell into their hands. And Cassius? floated
   like a butterfly—

Your name, a first narcotic,
lullaby droned to a girl

dozing in the slant light, the self
   souring

in its skin, and then she's carried
to the Sitz bath. Weary, tireless,

her Angel fingers his mortal
   Book,

where each ranked name
mouths the dead charm

that Joyce murmured stroking
   his novel:

Hoc est corpus meum.
Tree of the hand. Leaf and bloodvein.

Better to own a meaning
   not your own:

Redd Foxx (a grey Black man)
or *El Infanta de Castile*

reborn as Elephant and Castle:
   no finding her

in the Tube, drab girl
blanching for the stonecarvers—

And no finding that cancerous girl,
   for a rabbi

renames her; the Angel, misreading,
wanders the corridors lost.

Let the dying grow out of their words,
   me me me,

dear declining Diva, dear Lady
Bug. "When told by reporters

that it was King Hussein of
   Jordan,

and not Michael Jordan who had died,
a dazed Mariah [Carey] was led away . . . ."

*

Then the ledger rewrites itself,
    the Angel

hustles back to the girl's bed, fretful,
late, panting his devotions.

Hocus pocus. Here is my body.

Notes

The epigraphs for parts I, II, and III are derived from *The New Union Prayer Book,* p. 459; Jonah is the reading for Yom Kippur, the Day of Atonement.

"See Saw": "'The farmer looped . . . ,'" is based on a death near Ann Arbor, Michigan, around 1972. "The woman arrested for resisting arrest" refers to Sister Boom-Boom, San Francisco activist and perennial mayoral candidate of the early 1980s. *"Domine"* is from Monty Python's film, *Quest for the Holy Grail.* For "The man pinned . . . ," see Ken Kesey's novel, *Sometimes a Great Notion;* "the axe-man whispers *run"* refers to an apparent practice in medieval Europe.

"Gag": The passage beginning "surgeon drags / his son" is based on a scene from Woody Allen's film *Bananas.*

"Jacopone: The Scissors": In 1268, Jacopo dei Benedetti, a fashionable lawyer in the Tuscan town of Todi, pulled his mortally wounded wife, Vanna, from a collapsed banquet platform and found that she wore a hair-shirt under her gown. After undergoing a conversion, he lived as a ragged penitent in Todi and later joined the Franciscans. Known as Jacopone, he wrote over 90 poems called "Lauds," considered "the most powerful religious poetry in Italy before Dante's time." See *Jacopone da Todi's Lauds,* xix (trans. Serge Hughes and Elizabeth Hughes, New York: Paulist Press, 1982). This is a free version of Laud 38.

"*Chai:* 1924–2000": Some phrases refer to Yehuda Amichai's poems "Inside the Apple" and "North of San Francisco."

"Tacitus: City of Unseens": I have drawn from Tacitus's *Annals of Imperial Rome* (trans. Michael Grant), depicting the reign of Tiberius Caesar (14–37AD).

"One-Page Novel": "*Je reste . . . ,*" is from Louis Aragon's poem, "Richard II Quarante."

"Convolvulus, a Lullaby": *The Language of Flowers,* by Margaret Pickston (London: Michael Joseph, 1968).

"Redd-Pound Slamma": Furthermore, in the *Washington Post,* September 1, 2001, C3: "District officials said that clerical errors kept a deaf, mute and mentally ill man in the D.C. jail for nearly two years after charges against him were dismissed. Joseph S. Heard, 42, was a model prisoner, officials said. Reached at his new home, St. Elizabeths Hospital, Heard said, 'I do not know why I stayed in jail.'" For *"recumbent/mannequin,"* see E. Fuller Torrey, *The Roots of Treason: Ezra Pound and the Secret of St. Elizabeths,* pp. 203–4 (New York: McGraw-Hill, 1984): "Dr. Dalmau suggested that by lying on the floor Pound might have been imitating the Dadaist Barrès 'trial' where the defendant had been represented by a recumbent mannequin." "I broke—my head" is a quotation from Pound in Torrey, p. 202. *"This is a world of books..."* is from Elizabeth Bishop's poem "Visits to St. Elizabeths."

"Jacopone: House": This is a free version of Laud 77; see also note to "Jacopone: The Scissors."

"The Loop: JFK Jr": According to William Langewiesche's essay "The Turn," in *Inside the Sky: A Meditation on Flight* (New York: Pantheon, 1998), inexperienced pilots, who because of poor visibility cannot see the horizon, may misjudge that the plane is turning; if they then try to correct by turning, they can put themselves into a "graveyard spiral": "Pilots steer to the left just when they should steer to the right, and then in confusion they steer harder."

"Jacopone: On the Cobbles": See note to "Jacopone: The Scissors."

"Hocus Pocus": See *OED:* "magical formula coined by vagrant students"; "allusion to assumed derivation from *hoc est corpus meum.*" Mariah Carey is quoted in *USA Today,* February 8, 1999. The term "blood diary . . ." alludes to Witold Gombrowicz's *Diary,* (Evanston, Ill.: Northwestern University Press, 1988), which begins, "Monday Me. Tuesday Me. Wednesday Me. Thursday Me." The Ångström wavelength of light is named for physicist Anders Ångström; Sylvester Graham, minister and vegetarian, invented Graham Crackers; Cassius Clay is the given name of heavyweight boxing champion Muhammad Ali; Adam Ant refers to the new wave rocker; and Redd Foxx, comedian. For "the poet Cinna," see *Julius Caesar* III.iii.33–4: "It is no matter, his name's Cinna. Pluck but his name out of his heart, and turn him going." "Elephant and Castle" refers to London's Elephant and Castle tube station that is said to derive its name from Eleanor of Castile (el Infanta de Castile, 1246–1290), queen to England's King Edward I.